Dear Mum
PAM AYRES

D0888431

Dear Mum
Poems For Mums & Their Babies

PAM AYRES

Illustrated by Brian Reading

PEAUDOUCE

This exclusive Peaudouce edition published in 1985 by
SEVERN HOUSE PUBLISHERS LTD of
4 Brook Street, London W1Y 1AA

Typeset by South Bucks Photosetters Ltd., Beaconsfield, Bucks
Printed and bound by Anchor Brendon Ltd, Tiptree, Essex.

CONTENTS

The Pregnancy Poem

Dear Mum, I have achieved the state
Of pregnancy at last, I know you thought that I
Had let my chances fritter past
I know you had despaired
Of seeing any child of mine
But Mother! I have cracked it
At the age of ninety-nine!

I'm diligently going to
The ante-natal classes
They've issued me a card
To get me free false teeth and glasses
They've got a practice baby
You can bath and put to bed
It's only made of rubber
You can drop it on its head.

I'm taking vitamins
In case my diet is in doubt
I'm taking Brewers Yeast
To stop my hair from falling out
I'm drinking pints of milk
Because the calcium they say
Will give him mighty fangs
As he goes gnashing on his way.

I'm eating meat and fish and eggs
And bread with wholemeal flour
And every afternoon
I put me feet up for an hour
I practise relaxation
To reduce the labour pains
And wear elastic stockings
To unvaricose me veins.

And while I'm on the subject
What a bosom! What a chest
As fine a set of Bristols
As ever filled a vest
I don't deny at times
I might have liked a little more
But Mother! What a mantelpiece!
Now it's 44!

I've bought a fancy pram
In which to push him round the place
I'm rigging up a net
To keep the cat from off his face
I've bought a safety harness
So he cannot up and flee
When he's looking for his Mother
And he notices it's me.

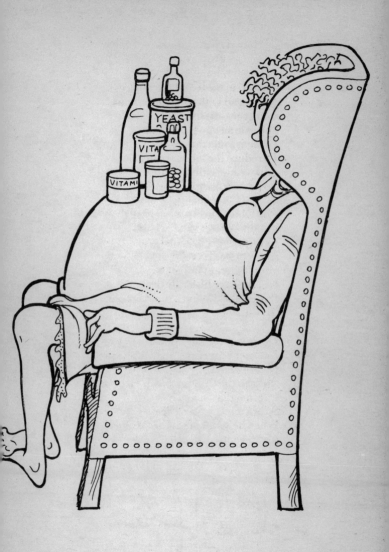

You asked me how I am, Mum
And I mustn't carry on
I'm not sick every morning
And the rash is nearly gone
I get a bit of backache
And me ankles tend to swell
But apart from heartburn, cramp
And sleepless nights, I'm very well.

Well Mum, that's all for now
Because I've got so much to do
And every twenty minutes
I am rushing to the ... garden
I thought I'd write a letter
Just to tell you how I am
From me, your everloving daughter
Pregnant Poet Pam.

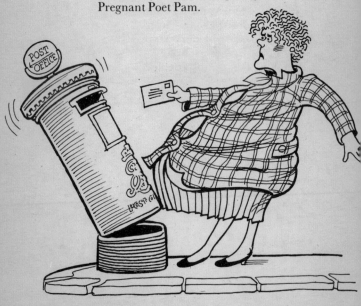

Wringing the Changes

I am studying the bottom
Of the boy I love the best
Lying on the carpet
Wearing nothing but his vest
Studying his antics
With a great maternal pride
As he wriggles and he pulls
And tries to reach the other side.

But suddenly a shadow falls
On this contented scene
The modern Mum's dilemma
How to keep her baby clean
Should it be with terry nappies
Freshly washed each day
Or should I use disposables
The ones you throw away?

Racked with indecision
By the glowing fire we sit
There's the tiny bottom
But who best to care for it?
I want no spots to blight it
Nothing tight to rudely chafe
But how to ward off nappy rash
And keep a bottom safe?

Take a terry nappy
Now it's very nice at first
But after every accident
It has to be immersed
In a nappy sanitizer
Which will slaughter every germ
In a mighty steaming bucket
That plays havoc with your perm.

And then I have to launder
Rinse, and hang it out to dry
Very nice providing that
The sun is in the sky
But if there is no sun
Nor any breeze to sweetly blow
Sopping in the basket
Back the nappies have to go.

I drape them round the kitchen
In an endless steaming chain
Or tumble dry them all
Which costs me twice as much again
Or hang them on a clothes horse
In the hope that they will air
And the dog goes rushing past
And gives them all a coat of hair.

And are they really comfortable?
This washing every day
Turned my fluffy nappies
Somewhat thin and hard and grey
Shall I fold a triangle?
Shall I fold a kite?
Or fold it in a cocked hat
In the middle of the night?

And then to seal him in
And waterproof the operation
I get the plastic pants
Which will prevent evaporation
I pop them on or pull them on
Or knot them front and back
And soon they get very stiff
And have a tendency to crack

So if I bought disposables
Would I be better off?
Would the purchase price
Cause me to stagger back and cough?
I'd not need terries, liners
Lidded buckets, soap and pegs
But would the massive cartons
Make me buckle at the legs?

And then at changing time
Would I feel joy and exultation
To see the cast-off nappy
Undergo incineration
To drop it in the dustbin
Turn around and skip away
And never more to ask
"Oh will the nappies dry today?"

Terries or disposables
Which sort shall I use?
Resealable? Elasticated?
Which one shall I choose?
To cater for the bottom
Of the boy I love the best
Lying on the carpet
Wearing nothing but his vest.

Mirror Song

Who's that boy in the mirror?
Who can that little boy be?
He's always there when I'm there
And he looks a lot like me
Oh
When I wear my blue trousers
He wears his too
And that little boy's Mummy
She looks a lot like you.

Where Did You Get . . ?

Where did you get a little round tum like that from?
Where did you get a little round tum like that from?
Mum's and Dad's are not like that
Mum's and Dad's are nice and flat
So where did you get a little round tum
A little round tum like yours?

and

Where did you get two little teeth like that from?
Where did you get two little teeth like that from?
Not one bit like Mummy or Dad
Mum's and Dad's teeth all went bad
So where did you get two little teeth
Two little teeth like yours?

and

Where did you get a sticky little face like that from?
Where did you get a sticky little face like that from?
The stickiest face I've ever seen
Mummy's and Dad's are nice and clean
So where did you get a sticky little face
A sticky little face like yours?

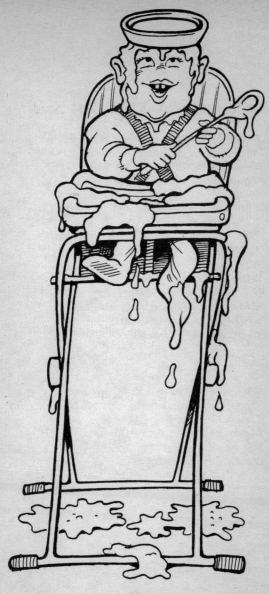

Before and After

Once I was a looker and so was my spouse
I recall when we first came to live in this house
He was young, optimistic and fresh in the face
With never the twang of a hernia brace.

He said he would die if he could not be mine
He wooed me with words more addictive than wine
The monastery beckoned, he wanted no other
But now he troops in and he says "Ulloo Mother".

He'd bound through the door with a laugh and a slap
And I used to think "My, there's a handsome young
  chap
Thank Heavens I'm wed to a red-blooded man"
But now I get pecks like you'd give your old Gran.

He used to take pains with the look of his hair
The top London salons, they all knew him there
No end ever split and no high standard slid
Now he goes round to George who'll oblige for a quid.

But when he first courted me, wasn't I proud
His gay repartee had me laughing out loud
But now he reclines in his jersey and socks
And in my direction grunts "What's on the box?"

I used to look on as he walked down the street
A picture of style from his head to his feet
But now there's a cap where the tresses have thinned
And faded old trousers that flap in the wind.

Mind I'm not blameless, I know very well
That the strain of maternity's starting to tell
I do what I can but there's one thing for sure
The mirror is no friend of mine any more.

He used to admire my refinement and poise
I'd turn up my nose at a smell or a noise
But now when I'm shouting he ducks with the rest
As I go haring past with a po and a vest.

Oh yes he admired the cut of my jib
And wasn't I thin? You could see every rib
But now in the chrome at the top of the cooker
I see many things, but I can't see a looker.

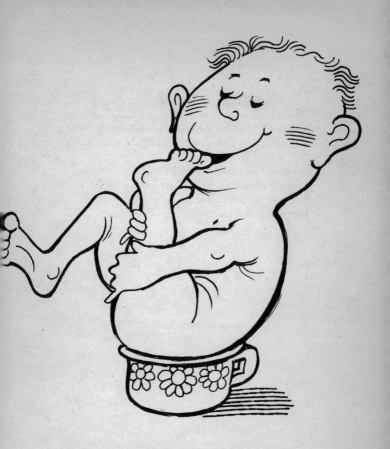

Whose Toes Are Those?

Whose toes are those?
Mine I suppose
And fingers, what luck!
I'll give them a suck.

Tiger, Tiger

The tiger that stalks through the night
Delivers a hideous bite
And there on his paws
Are hideous claws
But apart from all that, he's all right!

Mummy's Darling

You're the sweetest little baby
Mummy's ever seen
From top to toe
And at all points in between
From the funny soft spot
On your little bald head
To the great big burp
When you've just been fed.

There are all sorts of things
I could do, you know
I could go on the town
I could go and see a show
But for one gummy smile
And a gurgle or two
I think
    I'll stay
       by the fire
          with you.

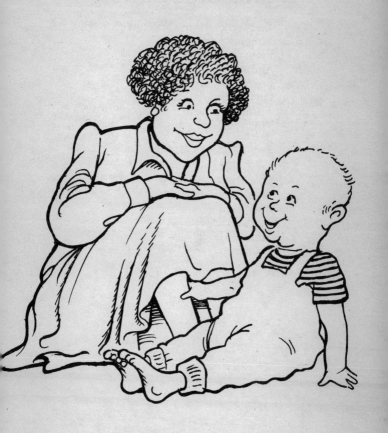

Aerobics

Well Mother, did I make a fool of myself
Last night on the bathroom floor
I'm so out of shape so I put on the tape
That I sent to the TV for
Well on came Felicity Kendal
With advice to be careful and slow
But I thought I knew best, I flung off me vest
And I thought "Right-o Mother, let's go!"

I bought my John McEnroe trainers
My, how expensive they've grown
But the thing with this pair is if I'm not there
They can run round the block on their own.
I borrowed your leotard, Mother
The one that enhances my charms
Thanks very much but it went at the crutch
When I started rotating my arms.

Then I did bicycling exercises
Flat out at a furious pace
All that went wrong was the dog came along
And licked up the side of me face
I bought Jane Fonda's book of Aerobics
I read it all morning in bed
It said "Go for the burn!"
There was that much to learn
That I went for a hot dog instead.

I bought my dear husband a tracksuit
He said terry towelling is best
With a curl of his lip he did up the zip
And took all the hair off his chest
We thought we might go on a fun run
We went with a very nice bloke
He'd not run before and he won't any more
'Cause they carted him off with a stroke.

But my dance record had novel methods
Special workouts and routines
It said I would get a superb silhouette
When I'm walking away in me jeans
And the music was truly inspiring
You wanted to give it what for
Flat on your back with your knees going crack
As the draught whistled under the door.

But Mother, I have to admit it
I went like a bull at a gate
I did it too fast, me legs couldn't last
And now I am sorry too late
I'm stiff and I'm over extended
It's agony, getting about
Thanks for the chance to be in the next dance
But I think I might sit this one out.

Buggy Ride Song

We're going for a buggy ride
Now what d'you think of that
We're going for a buggy ride
But you'll have to wear your hat
We're going for a buggy ride
What more can we do
If I push the buggy
Then the buggy pushes you.

Bottoms Up!

My Mummy crept up and washed me
I never had time to complain
She was under my shawl
With a cotton wool ball
And by CRIKEY! She's done it again.

I was lying in watery splendour
In a nappy so warm and so wet
When my mother crept up and washed me
And I haven't got over it yet!

Does a boy have no choice in the matter?
Can't a boy call his bottom his own?
No! She pulls down the sheet, gets hold of my feet
And she *won't* leave my bottom alone.

Foghorn Lullaby

Go to sleep my little foghorn
Give your poor old throat a rest
Of all the little foghorns
You're the one I love the best
You're the dearest little foghorn
In the country or the town
But how I sometimes wish
That I could turn the volume down!

Pat-a-cake

Pat-a-cake, Pat-a-cake
Baker's man
Bake us a cake
As fast as you can
But wash your hands
Before you invite us
'Cause we don't want
Gastro-enteritis!

Poor Dad

My wife was a lovely girl
A friend right from the start
We had good times together
Never cared to be apart
We went on lovely holidays
But now all that's gone west
For my wife's had a baby
And I am second best.

She won't come to the pictures
And she won't come for a drink
She's making eggy bread
Or washing bottles in the sink
She will not take my hand
Although I am the man she loves
No, she's nappy sterilizing
In a set of rubber gloves.

Either she is feeding him
Or tickling his tum
Patting him or stroking him
Or trying to suck his thumb
Then there's great excitement
When she holds him on the pot
I think if he performed
She'd have convulsions on the spot.

And when at last she's laid him
Tenderly into his cot
There he lies surrounded
By the trappings he has got
And leaning over all
I see the back view of his mother
Cranking up a mobile
Playing something or the other.

And hanging in his cot
He has a finger practice thing
And if he pokes or prods it
It will whirr and bonk and ding
At half past four each morning
Not a morning has he missed
He whirrs and bonks and dings
And drives his father round the twist.

And all across the carpet
Where I used to stretch me legs
Are his rattles, and his beakers
And his half chewed Bickiepegs
His pram, his little buggy
With the sunshade for his head
No don't tidy up
I'll go and sit out in the shed.

Last night for example
I had just come in from work
I'm glad no one was watching
Or I should have felt a berk
I burst in through the door
And I was throttled as I came
By the cables of a baby bouncer
Hanging from the frame.

He *is* a lovely baby
Anyone can plainly see
But while I'm fond of him
He hasn't got much time for me
Frankly as a Dad
I feel a failure and a dunce
When I appear he cries
And sicks and widdles all at once.

She's locked the bathroom cabinet
She's making such a fuss
I have to pick the padlock
Just to get me shaving brush
His little pots and bottles
Are clustered round the tap
For soothing gums and tums and bums
And nasty cradle cap.

I mustn't wake the baby up
Or give the door a slam
I mustn't mow the lawn
Because he's out there in his pram
I mustn't play my records
She's got noises on the brain
It's "Must you blow your nose?"
And "Did you *have* to pull the chain?"

Ah well, I've had me sandwich
So I'll clear off down the pub
I doubt my wife will notice
For they've both got in the tub
There's laughing and there's splashing
A good time's being had
"Well bye bye dear!"
Oh. She can't hear
"Try not to miss me . . . Dad".

Chillyfoot Indians

A tribe of Chillyfoot Indians
Came galloping over the plain
They'd all forgotten their socks and so
Their feet were chilly again.

They all rode Chillybottom ponies
Across the hills and dales
And they're called Chillybottom ponies
'Cause they've all forgotten their tails!

Mother's Day

The day our nanny got the sack
The baby slipped up round the back
Bumped his head and grazed his knee
And ran to her and not to me.

Dinner Time

It's time to have my dinner
Half past twelve has come
My shouting and complaining
Has proved too much for Mum
It might be Bovril soldiers
Or egg and bacon tart
It might be mashed banana
But it's time to make a start.

Mum puts me in my high chair
And stands it by the wall
She gets the bib and harness
And the suction plate and all
I push my feet against the table
Not too low or high
So the chair goes over backwards
And I bump my head and cry.

And then I get impatient
And rattle on my plate
And struggle in my high chair
So that Mum gets in a state
I take my teacher beaker
And whirl it by the spout
With any luck the lid comes off
And all the drink flies out.

Mum's keen on table manners
If a visitor has come
It's always "Sit up nicely now"
and "Eat it up for Mum"
So what I like to do
Is take a mouthful of the food
And smiling at the guest
I let it tumble out half-chewed.

Some I suck and swallow
Some I suck and leave
Some sticks in me hair
And quite a lot sticks on me sleeve
Mum gets irritated
When I give the bowl a stir
So before she takes my spoon away
I stick a bit on her.

Mummy's had no dinner
She's not looking very bright
She's looking very tired
Still I grizzled half the night
Her eyelids keep on closing
Her chin is on her chest
Of all the things we do each day
My Mum likes dinner time best.

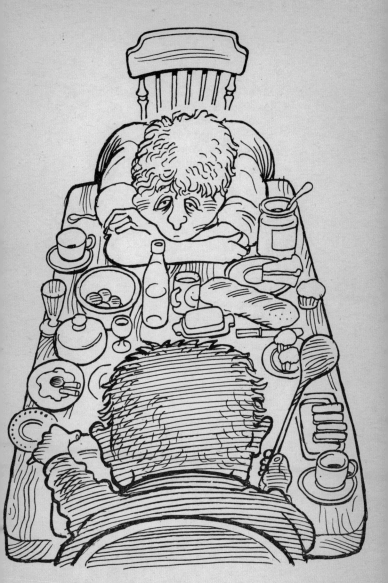

Wayne

My baby's eyes are bluer than yours
He's got much more hair and he's stronger
He's ever so bright
He sleeps through the night
And of our two I'd say mine is longer
I swear it's the truth
Mine's cutting a tooth
And he's obviously going to be tall
No, it's hard to explain
Now I've looked at your Wayne
Why *you* bothered to have one at all.

The Ballad of the Bungleclud

In the marshes, thick with mud
Lies the dreadful Bungleclud
In the bog up to his eyes
There he watches, there he spies
Still, except for fingers drumming
Looking out for people coming.

Bunglecluds are large and hairy
And their eyes are quick and wary
Watching out for signs of joggers
Ice-cream men or stray hot-doggers
English teachers, you or me
Or anyone to have for tea.

Bunglecluds are dark and wrinkled
And their tails are long and crinkled
On their ears are tufts of hair
That twitch and flicker everywhere
And both their nostrils red and flared
Are good for making people scared.

But oh, his mouth so wide and black
With great big tonsils down the back
And jagged teeth from left to right
No fillings, caps or crowns in sight
And Bunglebreath so foul and smelly
Turns most people's knees to jelly.

Lying in the mud so long
Causes Bunglecluds to pong
When it gets too much to bear
Up they get and out they tear
Climbing madly up the trees
To have an airing in the breeze.

When Bunglecluds no longer hum
Down to earth refreshed, they come
They promenade along the grass
And to Bunglecluds they pass
Enquire "How is your sainted Mother?"
And sweetly smile at one another.

Bunglecluds are rarely seen
But anywhere that mud is green
And deep and dark and nasty smelling
Go with caution! There's no telling!
Bubbles rising from the deep
Could mean a Bungleclud . . . Asleep!

Don't Start!

Hello Mum! We're here at last
Richard! Come and see!
Say "I'm nearly two now Gran"
I'd *love* a cup of tea
Not forgetting anything
That's the hardest part
RICHARD! Don't do that!
Get down! Come here! Sit still! Don't start!

We had to come this morning
It's the only chance we've got
Dad will need the car this week
He's travelling a lot
He sold the van!
He advertised it in Exchange and Mart
RICHARD! Put that back! Don't touch!
Now then! D'you hear! Don't start!

How's your ear? No better?
Have it syringed Mum, go today
I had mine syringed in April
I fell over all that day
We didn't have the dog put down
I didn't have the heart
DON'T YOU PUT THAT IN YOUR MOUTH
I'm warning you! Don't start!

You said you'd be a good boy
But I haven't seen it yet
Now look what Granny's given you
A little dartboard set
Don't just throw the paper down!
NO! DON'T YOU THROW THAT DART!
I'll knock your block off! Give it here!
Behave yourself! Don't start!

I've done the tea
Well, by this afternoon I'll start to flag
I've made us Gourmet Beef
I had to boil it in the bag
Dad likes a home made pudding
So I bought a Bakewell Tart
No you CAN'T HAVE SOME NOW!
Speak up! Don't answer back! Don't start!

What? Is that the time?
Half past eleven? What a shock!
Back we go then
Dad'll want the car for two o'clock
Look at all this junk
We should have brought a horse and cart
LOOK OUT! How many *more* times?
Now look what you've done! Don't start!

Say bye bye to Granny
And say thanks for having me
RICHARD! Kiss your Gran
Or you'll end up across my knee
She has NOT GOT WHISKERS Richard!
Don't you be so smart!
You thank her for a lovely time!
That's it! Bye Mum! Don't start!

Bonko Bonks

This is the story of Bonko Bonks
The finest boy in the land
All he would do when listening to you
Was suck the thumb on his hand
Well
One fine day poor Bonko Bonks
Choosing a peppermint lump
Found he had sucked his thumb clean away
And was only left with the stump!

One Mum to Another

Dear Mum, A little letter while the baby is asleep
I've tucked him in his cot and put the nappies in to steep
I took the bottle teat because his feeding seemed so slow
And stabbed it with a safety pin to quicken up the flow.

I haven't learned the knack of how to bath the baby yet
He seems to get so angry that he baths himself with
  sweat
And when I get him in it after dithering about
He widdles in the water and I have to take him out.

But if the days are difficult, the nights are harder still
I'm not one to complain but well perhaps today I will
I'm sleeping in my cosy bed and everything's all right
When a little hungry whimpering comes stealing
  through the night.

And off into the gloom we go, the baby and the mother
Slowly down the landing holding on to one another
I know he's only little and I know he must be fed
But I'd give a thousand pounds if I could jump back
  into bed.

You see I haven't had a decent sleep for weeks and weeks
But still I gamely dab the bottled roses on me cheeks
My lovely shiny hair that used to bounce about before
Is clogging up the hairbrush in the dressing table
  drawer.

I'm so tired Mother and my muscles seem so slack
They say that doing exercise will bring my figure back
My lovely tummy, flatter than the surface of a lake
Feels just like a plate of that blancmange you used
  to make.

So in the afternoon I have a nap, a little rest
An easy thing to do, a normal person would suggest
I curl up on the sofa with the papers on the floor
And half a dozen people start to hammer on the door.

Friends I haven't seen for years are there in overcoats
In they troop with coughs and colds and ulcerated
  throats
I have to give them cups of tea, I have to give them cake
And underneath my breath I think "Push off for
  goodness sake!"

I'll cook the dinner now and peg the nappies on the line
Mum, that's all for now but yes the babe and me are fine
I'd walk him in his pram but now it's gone in for repairs
For I'm afraid it got a rupture when I heaved it down
the stairs.

Love to everyone at home and will you tell them all
Thank you for the knitted coats. Every one's too small
I'll have to love and leave you, there is wailing from
on high
Did I make the right decision, Mother? Yes! Goodbye.